Name: _____

Address: _____

City/State/Zip: _____

Phone: _____

Email: _____

School: _____

School Address: _____

School Phone: _____

School Email: _____

Class Schedule/Teacher/Website/Email _____

Class 1 _____

Class 2 _____

Class 3 _____

Class 4 _____

Class 5 _____

Class 6 _____

Class 7 _____

Class 8 _____

Design by April Chloe Terrazas | © 2016 Crazy Brainz, LLC | **www.AprilChloeTerrazasAmazon.com**
ISBN#: 978-1-941775-32-5

	SCHEDULE FOR THE YEAR
7a	
8a	
9a	
10a	
11a	
12p	
1p	
2p	
3p	
4p	
5p	

Notes:

Time	SCHEDULE FOR THE YEAR
Morning	
Lunch	
Afternoon	

January	February	March	April	May	June
1 _____	1 _____	1 _____	1 _____	1 _____	1 _____
2 _____	2 _____	2 _____	2 _____	2 _____	2 _____
3 _____	3 _____	3 _____	3 _____	3 _____	3 _____
4 _____	4 _____	4 _____	4 _____	4 _____	4 _____
5 _____	5 _____	5 _____	5 _____	5 _____	5 _____
6 _____	6 _____	6 _____	6 _____	6 _____	6 _____
7 _____	7 _____	7 _____	7 _____	7 _____	7 _____
8 _____	8 _____	8 _____	8 _____	8 _____	8 _____
9 _____	9 _____	9 _____	9 _____	9 _____	9 _____
10 _____	10 _____	10 _____	10 _____	10 _____	10 _____
11 _____	11 _____	11 _____	11 _____	11 _____	11 _____
12 _____	12 _____	12 _____	12 _____	12 _____	12 _____
13 _____	13 _____	13 _____	13 _____	13 _____	13 _____
14 _____	14 _____	14 _____	14 _____	14 _____	14 _____
15 _____	15 _____	15 _____	15 _____	15 _____	15 _____
16 _____	16 _____	16 _____	16 _____	16 _____	16 _____
17 _____	17 _____	17 _____	17 _____	17 _____	17 _____
18 _____	18 _____	18 _____	18 _____	18 _____	18 _____
19 _____	19 _____	19 _____	19 _____	19 _____	19 _____
20 _____	20 _____	20 _____	20 _____	20 _____	20 _____
21 _____	21 _____	21 _____	21 _____	21 _____	21 _____
22 _____	22 _____	22 _____	22 _____	22 _____	22 _____
23 _____	23 _____	23 _____	23 _____	23 _____	23 _____
24 _____	24 _____	24 _____	24 _____	24 _____	24 _____
25 _____	25 _____	25 _____	25 _____	25 _____	25 _____
26 _____	26 _____	26 _____	26 _____	26 _____	26 _____
27 _____	27 _____	27 _____	27 _____	27 _____	27 _____
28 _____	28 _____	28 _____	28 _____	28 _____	28 _____
29 _____	29 _____	29 _____	29 _____	29 _____	29 _____
30 _____		30 _____	30 _____	30 _____	30 _____
31 _____		31 _____		31 _____	

July	August	September	October	November	December
1	1	1	1	1	1
2	2	2	2	2	2
3	3	3	3	3	3
4	4	4	4	4	4
5	5	5	5	5	5
6	6	6	6	6	6
7	7	7	7	7	7
8	8	8	8	8	8
9	9	9	9	9	9
10	10	10	10	10	10
11	11	11	11	11	11
12	12	12	12	12	12
13	13	13	13	13	13
14	14	14	14	14	14
15	15	15	15	15	15
16	16	16	16	16	16
17	17	17	17	17	17
18	18	18	18	18	18
19	19	19	19	19	19
20	20	20	20	20	20
21	21	21	21	21	21
22	22	22	22	22	22
23	23	23	23	23	23
24	24	24	24	24	24
25	25	25	25	25	25
26	26	26	26	26	26
27	27	27	27	27	27
28	28	28	28	28	28
29	29	29	29	29	29
30	30	30	30	30	30
31	31		31		31

July	August	September

October	November	December

July	August	September

January	February	March

April	May	June

Name	Email	Phone #

Name	Email	Phone #

Teacher Name	Teacher Website

MONTH:_____

Monday	Tuesday	Wednesday

MONTH:_____

Thursday	Friday	Saturday/Sunday

MONTH:_____

Monday	Tuesday	Wednesday

Monday	Tuesday	Wednesday

MONTH: _____

Thursday	Friday	Saturday/Sunday

MONTH:_____

Monday	Tuesday	Wednesday

MONTH:_____

Thursday	Friday	Saturday/Sunday

MONTH:_____

Monday	Tuesday	Wednesday

Monday	Tuesday	Wednesday

MONTH:_____

Thursday	Friday	Saturday/Sunday

MONTH:_____

Monday	Tuesday	Wednesday

MONTH:_____

Thursday	Friday	Saturday/Sunday

MONTH:_____

Monday	Tuesday	Wednesday

MONTH:_____

Thursday	Friday	Saturday/Sunday

MONTH:_____

Monday	Tuesday	Wednesday

MONTH:_____

Thursday	Friday	Saturday/Sunday

MONTH:_____

Monday	Tuesday	Wednesday

MONTH:_____

Thursday	Friday	Saturday/Sunday

MONTH:_____

Monday	Tuesday	Wednesday

MONTH:_____

Thursday	Friday	Saturday/Sunday

MONTH:_____

Monday	Tuesday	Wednesday

MONTH:_____

Thursday	Friday	Saturday/Sunday

MONTH:_____

Monday	Tuesday	Wednesday

MONTH:_____

Thursday	Friday	Saturday/Sunday

MONTH:_____

Monday	Tuesday	Wednesday

MONTH:_____

Thursday	Friday	Saturday/Sunday

Thursday	Friday	Saturday/Sunday

Important This Week

Goals

To Do

Day	Schedule	Homework	HW done
M			
T			
W			
Th			
F			

Projects/Tests

Important This Week

Goals

To Do

Day	Schedule	Homework	HW done
M			
T			
W			
Th			
F			

Projects/Tests

Important This Week

Goals

To Do

Week/Month:

Day	Schedule	Homework	HW done
M			
T			
W			
Th			
F			

Projects/Tests

Important This Week

Goals

To Do

Week/Month: Student Planner

Day	Schedule	Homework	HW done
M			
T			
W			
Th			
F			

Projects/Tests

Important This Week

Goals

To Do

Week/Month: Student Planner

Day	Schedule	Homework	HW done
M			
T			
W			
Th			
F			

Projects/Tests

Important This Week

Goals

To Do

Day	Schedule	Homework	HW done
M			
T			
W			
Th			
F			

Projects/Tests

Important This Week

Goals

To Do

Day	Schedule	Homework	HW done
M			
T			
W			
Th			
F			

Projects/Tests

Important This Week

Goals

To Do

Week/Month: _____   Student Planner

Day	Schedule	Homework	HW done
M			
T			
W			
Th			
F			

Projects/Tests

Important This Week

Goals

To Do

Day	Schedule	Homework	HW done
M			
T			
W			
Th			
F			

Projects/Tests

Important This Week

Goals

To Do

Day	Schedule	Homework	HW done
M			
T			
W			
Th			
F			

Projects/Tests

Important This Week

Goals

To Do

Day	Schedule	Homework	HW done
M			
T			
W			
Th			
F			

Projects/Tests

Important This Week

Goals

To Do

Day	Schedule	Homework	HW done
M			
T			
W			
Th			
F			

Projects/Tests

Important This Week

Goals

To Do

Day	Schedule	Homework	HW done
M			
T			
W			
Th			
F			

Projects/Tests

Important This Week

Goals

To Do

Day	Schedule	Homework	HW done
M			
T			
W			
Th			
F			

Projects/Tests

Important This Week

Goals

To Do

Week/Month: Student Planner

Day	Schedule	Homework	HW done
M			
T			
W			
Th			
F			

Projects/Tests

Important This Week

Goals

To Do

Day	Schedule	Homework	HW done
M			
T			
W			
Th			
F			

Projects/Tests

Important This Week

Goals

To Do

Day	Schedule	Homework	HW done
M			
T			
W			
Th			
F			

Projects/Tests

Important This Week

Goals

To Do

Day	Schedule	Homework	HW done
M			
T			
W			
Th			
F			

Projects/Tests

Important This Week

Goals

To Do

Day	Schedule	Homework	HW done
M			
T			
W			
Th			
F			

Projects/Tests

Important This Week

Goals

To Do

Day	Schedule	Homework	HW done
M			
T			
W			
Th			
F			

Projects/Tests

Important This Week

Goals

To Do

Day	Schedule	Homework	HW done
M			
T			
W			
Th			
F			

Projects/Tests

Important This Week

Goals

To Do

Day	Schedule	Homework	HW done
M			
T			
W			
Th			
F			

Projects/Tests

Important This Week

Goals

To Do

Day	Schedule	Homework	HW done
M			
T			
W			
Th			
F			

Projects/Tests

Important This Week

Goals

To Do

Day	Schedule	Homework	HW done
M			
T			
W			
Th			
F			

Projects/Tests

Important This Week

Goals

To Do

Day	Schedule	Homework	HW done
M			
T			
W			
Th			
F			

Projects/Tests

Important This Week

Goals

To Do

Week/Month:

Student Planner

Day	Schedule	Homework	HW done
M			
T			
W			
Th			
F			

Projects/Tests

Important This Week

Goals

To Do

Week/Month: Student Planner

Day	Schedule	Homework	HW done
M			
T			
W			
Th			
F			

Projects/Tests

Important This Week

Goals

To Do

Week/Month:

Day	Schedule	Homework	HW done
M			
T			
W			
Th			
F			

Projects/Tests

Important This Week

Goals

To Do

Day	Schedule	Homework	HW done
M			
T			
W			
Th			
F			

Projects/Tests

Important This Week

Goals

To Do

Day	Schedule	Homework	HW done
M			
T			
W			
Th			
F			

Projects/Tests

Important This Week

Goals

To Do

Day	Schedule	Homework	HW done
M			
T			
W			
Th			
F			

Projects/Tests

Important This Week

Goals

To Do

Day	Schedule	Homework	HW done
M			
T			
W			
Th			
F			

Projects/Tests

Important This Week

Goals

To Do

Day	Schedule	Homework	HW done
M			
T			
W			
Th			
F			

Projects/Tests

Important This Week

Goals

To Do

Day	Schedule	Homework	HW done
M			
T			
W			
Th			
F			

Projects/Tests

Important This Week

Goals

To Do

Day	Schedule	Homework	HW done
M			
T			
W			
Th			
F			

Projects/Tests

Important This Week

Goals

To Do

Day	Schedule	Homework	HW done
M			
T			
W			
Th			
F			

Projects/Tests

Important This Week

Goals

To Do

Day	Schedule	Homework	HW done
M			
T			
W			
Th			
F			

Projects/Tests

Important This Week

Goals

To Do

Day	Schedule	Homework	HW done
M			
T			
W			
Th			
F			

Projects/Tests

Important This Week

Goals

To Do

Day	Schedule	Homework	HW done
M			
T			
W			
Th			
F			

Projects/Tests

Important This Week

Goals

To Do

Week/Month:

Day	Schedule	Homework	HW done
M			
T			
W			
Th			
F			

Projects/Tests

Important This Week

Goals

To Do

Day	Schedule	Homework	HW done
M			
T			
W			
Th			
F			

Projects/Tests

Important This Week

Goals

To Do

Day	Schedule	Homework	HW done
M			
T			
W			
Th			
F			

Projects/Tests

Important This Week

Goals

To Do

Day	Schedule	Homework	HW done
M			
T			
W			
Th			
F			

Projects/Tests

Important This Week

Goals

To Do

Day	Schedule	Homework	HW done
M			
T			
W			
Th			
F			

Projects/Tests

Important This Week

Goals

To Do

Day	Schedule	Homework	HW done
M			
T			
W			
Th			
F			

Projects/Tests

Important This Week

Goals

To Do

Day	Schedule	Homework	HW done
M			
T			
W			
Th			
F			

Projects/Tests

Important This Week

Goals

To Do

Important This Week

Day	Schedule	Homework	HW done
M			
T			
W			
Th			
F			

Projects/Tests

Important This Week

Goals

To Do

Day	Schedule	Homework	HW done
M			
T			
W			
Th			
F			

Projects/Tests

Important This Week

Goals

To Do

Day	Schedule	Homework	HW done
M			
T			
W			
Th			
F			

Projects/Tests

Important This Week

Goals

To Do

Week/Month: Student Planner

Day	Schedule	Homework	HW done
M			
T			
W			
Th			
F			

Projects/Tests

Important This Week

Goals

To Do

Day	Schedule	Homework	HW done
M			
T			
W			
Th			
F			

Projects/Tests

Important This Week

Goals

To Do

Day	Schedule	Homework	HW done
M			
T			
W			
Th			
F			

Projects/Tests

Important This Week

Goals

To Do

Day	Schedule	Homework	HW done
M			
T			
W			
Th			
F			

Projects/Tests

Important This Week

Goals

To Do

Week/Month: Student Planner

Day	Schedule	Homework	HW done
M			
T			
W			
Th			
F			

Projects/Tests

Important This Week

Goals

To Do

Day	Schedule	Homework	HW done
M			
T			
W			
Th			
F			

Projects/Tests

www.ingramcontent.com/pod-product-compliance
Lightning Source LLC
LaVergne TN
LVHW070841080426

835513LV00024B/2424

9 781941 775325